FUNDS TO PURCHASE
THIS BOOK WERE
PROVIDED BY A
40TH ANNIVERSARY GRANT
FROM THE
FOELLINGER FOUNDATION.

ANIMALS BY HABITAT

ANIMALS
OF THE
RAIN FOREST

STEPHEN SAVAGE

RSVP

RAINTREE
STECK-VAUGHN
PUBLISHERS
The Steck-Vaughn Company

Austin, Texas

Titles in the Animals by Habitat series
Animals of the Desert
Animals of the Grasslands
Animals of the Oceans
Animals of the Rain Forest

Published by Raintree Steck-Vaughn Publishers, an imprint of Steck-Vaughn Company

Library of Congress Cataloging-in-Publication Data
Savage, Stephen.
Animals of the rainforest / Stephen Savage.
     p.   cm.—(Animals by habitat)
     Includes bibliographical references and index.
     Summary: Describes the environment of the rain forest and some of the birds, mammals, amphibians, and reptiles that live there.
     ISBN 0-8172-4751-3
     1. Rain forest animals—Juvenile literature.
     2. Rain forest ecology—Juvenile literature.
     3. Rain forests—Juvenile literature.
     [1. Rain forest animals. 2. Rain forests.]
     I. Title. II. Series: Savage, Stephen, 1965- Animals by habitat.
     QL112.S29 1997
     591.909'52—dc20   96-31740

Printed in Italy. Bound in the United States.
1 2 3 4 5 6 7 8 9 0 01 00 99 98 97

Habitat Maps
The habitat maps in this series show the general distribution of each animal at a glance.

Picture Acknowledgments
Ardea London Ltd Adrian Warren 7 (top) and 27 (bottom), Wardene Weisser 25 (top); **Bruce Coleman Ltd** Alain Compost 13 (top), Francisco J Erize 7 (bottom), MPL Fogden 14 and 25 (bottom), Michael Freeman 9 (top), CB & DW Frith 5 (inset), Stephen J Krasemann 27 (top), Luiz Claudio Marigo 18, Dr John Mackinnon 17 (top), Mike McKavett 19 (bottom), Dr Norman Myers 23 (top), Dieter & Mary Plage 16, Hector Rivarola 29 (top), Leonard Lee Rue 19 (top) and 21 (top), Kim Taylor 22 and 28, Carl Wallace cover left cutout (TBC), Rod Williams 11 (bottom), Konrad Wothe 12; **Frank Lane Picture Agency** Silvestris 23 (bottom), Terry Whittaker 4; **NHPA** 21 (bottom), Stephen Dalton 9 (bottom); **OSF** Doug Allan 15 (bottom), Stephen Dalton 17 (bottom), Richard Davies 29 (bottom), Michael Fogden 10 and cover, 24, Michael Leach 26, John Netherton cover right cutout (TBC), Ronald Toms 5 (main), Belinda Wright 11 (top); **OSF (Animals Animals)** John Stern (top) 15; **OSF (Survival Anglia)** Dr F Köster 20; **Zefa** 13 (bottom).

Contents

Words that are printed in **bold** in the text are explained in the glossary on pages 30–31.

Introduction

Rain forests are areas of dense forest found in parts of the world where there is heavy rainfall. This **habitat** is home to more animals and plants than any other. Down on the forest floor it is hot, steamy, and quiet. The few **mammals** that live there are shy and always on the lookout for danger. Many live in pairs and call to each other softly so they do not attract a **predator**. Others, like the tapir, wander through the forest alone. Then there are the big cats, the strong, silent hunters.

High above the ground the leafy branches form a vast green **canopy**. This is where most rain forest creatures live. The branches link together, forming pathways that monkeys and other animals use to travel through the thick forest. Up there, it is light and much cooler.

Nearer the ground the sounds of parrots, monkeys, frogs, and insects echo through the forest. Dawn and dusk are often the noisiest times of the day. Every morning groups of monkeys call to warn other monkeys that they are on the move. Howler monkeys are the loudest land animals, but even their calls are drowned out by the constant downpour during a forest storm.

Tropical rain forests are rich in ▶ animal life, but most of the wildlife is hidden from view.

The tapir is one of several **herbivores** ▶ that live on the forest floor. It uses its short trunk to pull leaves and twigs into its mouth.

Sadly, many rain forest animals are in danger of becoming **extinct**. Tigers and jaguars are killed for their fur, and parrots are caught as pets. Because we cut down the forest for wood and use the land for farming, the world's rain forests are shrinking, endangering the rain forest animals and the forest itself.

▲ The future of the world's rain forests is in our hands.

Rain Forests of the World

Tropical rain forests grow in hot parts of the world near the equator. This area includes parts of South America, Africa, eastern Madagascar, and southern Asia. The rain forests of today are the small remains of much larger ancient forests. The vast rain forests survived the Ice Age, which began 700,000 years ago. It is thought that more than two thirds of the world's animals and plants live in rain forests. The trees and plants of the rain forest help to produce the air we breathe by giving off large amounts of oxygen.

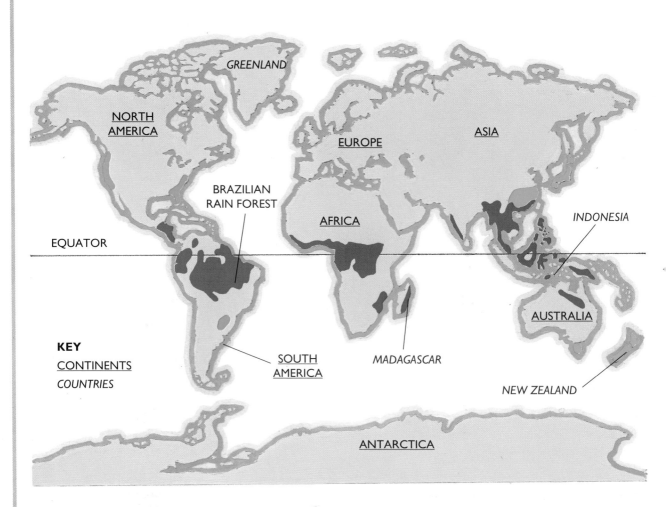

▲ The world's remaining major rain forests. Tropical rain forests are shown in red, and temperate rain forests are shown in green.

African cloud forest, home to the ▶
magnificent mountain gorilla

There are several different types of tropical rain forest created by the **climate** and geography of the land. In some countries, more than one type of rain forest is found. In South America and Africa, there are areas of lowland evergreen forest as well as areas of cloud forest in the higher regions that draw most of their moisture from large clouds of ghostly mist.

Another type of tropical rain forest is the highland forest, which grows on mountain slopes. This type of forest is stunted and is made up of much smaller trees and shrubs than is the lowland forest.

The tropical **monsoon** forests of southern Asia have six months of rain followed by six months of dry weather. These extreme weather conditions are caused by the seasonal monsoon winds.

A small part of the world's rain forest is found not in the tropical but in the temperate regions.

Temperate forests receive enough rainfall to be classified as rain forests but are found in warm, not hot, climates. Unlike tropical rain forests, they have well-defined seasons throughout the year. The main temperate rain forests are in North America, New Zealand, eastern Asia, and Japan.

The prickly porcupine lives in ▶
the temperate rain forest
of North America.

The Rain Forest Habitat

The rain forest can be divided into three different parts: the canopy, the understory, and the forest floor. If you could look down on a rain forest, you would see a blanket of green. This is the forest canopy, formed by the leaves and branches of the tallest trees nearly 100 feet from the ground. A few tall, narrow trees, called **emergents**, manage to grow above the canopy.

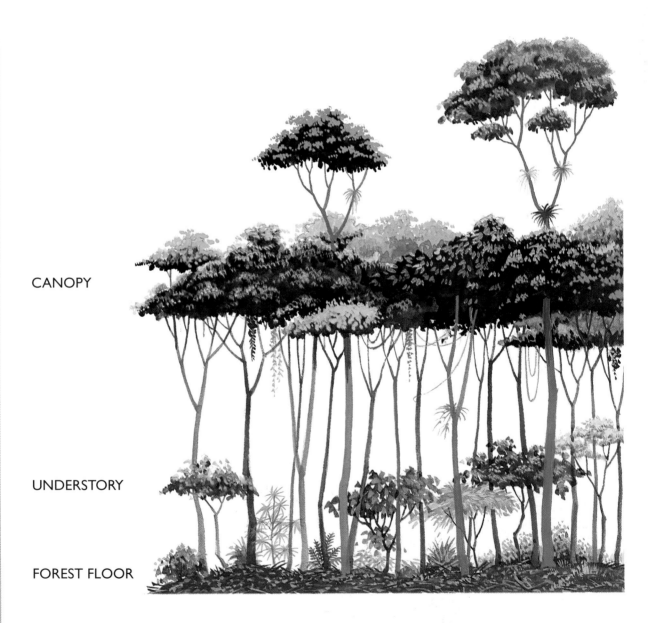

CANOPY

UNDERSTORY

FOREST FLOOR

▲ The three layers of a rain forest

▲ Two thirds of the Earth's fresh water is in the Amazon rain forest; this includes the Amazon River, which is 3,968 miles long.

There are many splashes of color among the green leaves in the sunlit canopy. These are the colorful, scented flowers produced by the trees and the forest plants that grow on them. The colors and scents attract insects, birds, and even monkeys to **pollinate** the flowers of the trees and plants.

Below the canopy is the understory, the tops of smaller trees that form another layer. Many young trees stretch upward in a race to reach the sunlight. This layer is also home to various monkeys, snakes, birds, and frogs.

The forest floor is covered by a layer of leaves. As they **decay**, these leaves give off **nutrients** that plants take into their roots as food. The forest floor is home to many **invertebrates** that feed on the decaying leaves. It is also home to a few herbivore mammals and the **carnivores** that hunt them.

Some large rivers, including the Zaire in Africa and the Amazon in South America, flow through rain forests. These provide a home for some animals and drinking and bathing water for others. The Amazon River is home to many fish, including the tambaqui, which eats fruit that has fallen into the river. In the rainy season, parts of the Amazon rain forest become flooded, and the forest floor becomes a feeding ground for fish.

◄ Like many hummingbirds, the amazilia hummingbird feeds on nectar from forest flowers.

Mammals

The main predators in the forest are the big cats. When a big cat is hunting, the other jungle animals are silent. Most jungle cats have two to four cubs. Tiger and jaguar cubs are reared by the mother alone. When they are a few months old, the cubs follow their mother on hunting trips until they are old enough to look after themselves. Big cats spend most of their lives living alone.

Jaguar

The jaguar is the largest of the South American cats. Its spotted coat provides excellent **camouflage** when hunting forest mammals such as tapir, deer, or mice. A jaguar leaps at its **prey** with its claws extended from its large paws. It is an agile climber and also loves water. A jaguar sometimes catches fish by flipping them out of the water with its paw.

▲ A jaguar can climb in the lower branches of the understory, but more usually hunts on the forest floor.

▲ The striped colors of the tiger provide superb camouflage.

Indian tiger

Tigers have the most beautifully marked fur of all the big cats. This striped fur helps the tiger to blend in with the surrounding forest as it stalks its prey. Although very powerful, the tiger can chase its prey for only a short distance. It will usually leap from cover and kill its prey with one bite to the throat. Tigers eat large mammals such as buffalo and can kill an animal twice their own size. In hot weather, a tiger will often cool itself in a pool or stream.

Jaguarundi

The jaguarundi of South America is also known as the otter cat because of its otterlike features. This dark-colored cat grows to under three feet in length and has neither spots nor stripes. The jaguarundi is active during the day, but more active at night. It catches birds, small mammals, and fish and sometimes eats fruit. Unlike the jaguar and tiger, adult jaguarundis live in pairs.

▲ The jaguarundi is an agile hunter that prefers to catch ground birds.

Monkeys and apes are familiar rain forest dwellers. Many different types of monkey live in rain forests, where they eat, play, and sleep in the treetops. They live in groups for safety and rarely visit the forest floor. Monkeys groom each other, which helps to strengthen the bond between them. Most monkeys and apes eat leaves and fruit; in fact, they get most of their water by eating fruit.

Spider monkey

Black spider monkeys wander through the forest in search of food. Because of their body size (19.5 in.), they have little to fear from the eagles that hunt above the treetops. The spider monkey can hang onto a branch by its tail or even use it to pick up food. Spider monkeys drink nectar from flowers and carry pollen from one plant to another on their fur. They sometimes break off large branches and drop them on predators on the forest floor.

◀ Spider monkeys are so-called because of the agile way they move in the trees using their long, thin limbs.

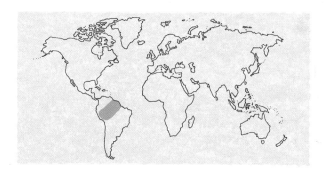

▲ Male orangutans have large cheek flaps and a throat pouch that they display to warn off other males.

Orangutan

Orangutans are apes, related to the African chimpanzee and gorilla. They usually live alone, slowly climbing through the forest in search of their favorite food—fruit. Orangutans use their long arms and legs for climbing or walking upright. They can even use their hands to drink water from a tree hole. The male orangutan grows twice as large as the female; in fact, it can be almost as tall as a man.

Colubus monkey

Baby black and white colubus monkeys are born completely white. When the baby monkey is two weeks old, it is able to cling onto its mother's back as she swings through the trees. Unlike the spider monkey, the colubus monkey cannot hang from a branch by its tail. The main enemies of colubus monkeys are eagles, leopards, and humans.

▲ The colubus monkey is unusual because it has only four fingers and no thumb on each hand.

MAMMALS

A part from cats and monkeys, the forest branches are home to other mammals, including the sloth, sun bear, and lemur. The 22 species of lemur, an animal like a monkey, are found only on the island of Madagascar.

Three-toed sloth

The three-toed sloth spends most of its life alone, hanging upside down in the canopy of the Amazon rain forest. It moves in slow motion and can take a day to travel from one tree to another. Sloths spend about 18 hours of each day asleep. They have poor hearing and eyesight, so they use smell and touch to find their leafy food. Sloths never groom themselves, and the damp climate causes green **algae** to grow in their fur. This green algae provides a camouflage as the sloth slowly passes through the trees.

◀ The sloth hangs from branches and vines using a special hooked claw on each limb.

▲ The sun bear gets its name from the orange marking on its chest.

Sun bear

The southeast Asian sun bear is the smallest type of bear, reaching only five feet in length. It spends much of the day asleep or sunbathing in a nest made from branches high up in the trees. Sun bears feed on fruit, termites, and occasionally small mammals and birds. They also love honey and use their claws to rip open bees' nests, scooping out the honey with their narrow tongues.

Indris

Like all lemurs, the indris is a relative of the monkey and ape. Indris live in small family groups and move around just below the canopy, leaping from tree trunk to tree trunk. They can easily leap distances of 16 feet, grasping the tree trunk with their large hands and feet as they land. The indris is active during the day, feeding on fruit and leaves. A newborn indris hangs onto its mother's fur, leaving the mother's hands free for climbing.

The indris, at three feet tall, is the largest of all the lemurs. ▼

A few types of mammal, such as bats and colugos, can actually fly or glide through the forest. The rain forest is home to many different types of bat, which feed on insects, small mammals, fruit, and nectar.

Indian flying fox

The Indian flying fox is one of the largest types of bat, with a wing span of five feet. Its wings are made of a leathery skin, which grows between the arm and finger bones. It feeds on fruit and drinks from rivers. The flying fox spends the day in a roost tree, which may contain hundreds or even thousands of other flying foxes. A baby flying fox spends the first few weeks clinging to its mother's body, even when she is flying.

▲ The flying fox hangs upside down from a branch by its feet and takes flight simply by letting go.

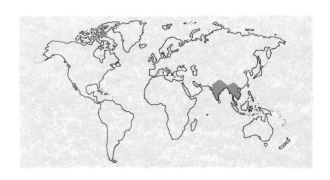

Vampire bat

The mouse-sized vampire bat feeds only on the blood of sleeping mammals such as domestic cattle, pigs, and, occasionally, humans. Vampire bats pierce their victims' skin with two sharp teeth. They then lap up the victim's blood while their saliva prevents the blood from clotting. A bat must drink half its body weight in blood each night and will die if it goes without food for more than two days. Vampire bats produce high-pitched sounds and avoid colliding with objects by listening for the echo of these sounds.

Colugo

The leaf-eating colugo glides through the forest. It has arms, legs, and a tail that are joined together by skin. As the colugo leaps from a tree, it spreads its arms and legs and sails through the air like a hang glider. It lands on the trunk of the nearest tree, climbs to the top, and leaps again. Colugos are active at night. They spend the day resting, their mottled fur camouflaging them against the bark of the trees.

▲ The colugo can easily glide more than 100 yards at a time.

▲ A vampire bat rarely drinks enough blood to harm its victim seriously.

Birds

The best known of all the forest birds is the parrot, of which there are 330 different types in the world. Most parrots have brightly colored feathers and fly through the forest like living rainbows. Parrots are also good climbers, which is why they are sometimes called "winged monkeys." Parrots share the forest canopy with the strange-looking toucan, identified by its large, colorful beak.

Toco toucan

The toco is the largest of 33 different kinds of toucan in the rain forest, reaching two feet in length. It uses its large beak to reach fruit growing on branches that would not be able to support its weight. It also eats small lizards and baby birds. The toucan never goes down to the forest floor. It bathes using rainwater that has collected in tree hollows.

▲ The toucan's brightly colored beak may be used to signal to other toucans.

▲ The scarlet macaw is one of the world's largest parrots, reaching three feet from its head to the tip of its tail.

Scarlet macaw

Like other parrots, the scarlet macaw has a large, tough beak for breaking open hard nuts and seeds. The hooked part of its beak is used for scooping out the flesh of soft fruit. Some fruits eaten by the scarlet macaw are poisonous. If this happens, the macaw then eats a special clay that stops the poison from harming it. Sometimes macaws live in groups of up to 20, feeding and flying together.

Ring-necked parakeet

Indian ring-necked parakeets usually live in noisy groups, except in the breeding season when they live in pairs. The male parakeet feeds the female and the newly hatched chicks for the first week. Ring-necked parakeets eat fruit, seeds, flowers, and nectar.

▲ Only the adult ring-necked parakeet has the attractive rose-colored neck markings.

M any other birds live in the rain forests, including the predatory eagle, the shy kiwi, and the unusual hoatzin. The wings of tiny hummingbirds hum as they dart among the **vegetation** like large, multicolored insects.

Hoatzin

The strange hoatzin bird prefers to live and nest in the lower branches of trees overhanging water. The female hoatzin lays two to four eggs that hatch after one month. The hoatzin is a poor flyer and sometimes crashes into vegetation when trying to land. The adult bird flies away from danger, but its chicks flee to safety by leaping into water and clawing their way onto land farther downstream. Like **prehistoric** birds, hoatzin chicks have a small claw on each wing that helps them climb through branches. These claws disappear after a few weeks.

◀ The hoatzin eats leaves, flowers, and sometimes small animals.

▲ The crowned hawk eagle is named after its large head crest.

Crowned hawk eagle

The crowned hawk eagle is the bird most feared by the inhabitants of the African rain forest. It feeds on a variety of mammals, lizards, and snakes, but small monkeys are its favorite prey. When an eagle circles above the treetops, the monkeys below are sent into a panic. The eagle must kill its prey immediately, using its powerful claws. If a struggling monkey damages the eagle's feathers, it may no longer be able to fly or hunt.

Brown kiwi

The flightless brown kiwi spends the day asleep, hidden among the undergrowth on the forest floor. Having good eyesight and sensitive whiskers around its beak, this bird has no problem finding its way around in the dark. The kiwi's large clawed feet can be used for running, digging, or defending its territory against intruders. Kiwis usually live in pairs. The female lays up to two eggs in a hole hidden in dense vegetation. The male incubates and guards the eggs for 11 weeks until the chicks hatch.

The brown kiwi has sensitive nostrils on the end of its beak for finding insects, earthworms, and fruits. ▼

Reptiles

The heat of the rain forest is ideal for **cold-blooded** animals, such as **reptiles,** because their body temperature is controlled by the surrounding air temperature. Many types of snake and lizard live and hunt in branches and on the forest floor.

Parson's chameleon

The parson's chameleon is perfectly adapted for life in the trees. Chameleons are masters of camouflage, changing color to

▲ A parson's chameleon shoots out its long, sticky tongue to catch its food.

blend in with their surroundings. They also change color to attract a mate or to warn off a rival. When hunting, a Parson's chameleon keeps still by holding onto a branch with its tail while its eyes move in opposite directions, searching for prey. The chameleon feeds mainly on insects.

▲ Green is the perfect skin color for the tree-living Congo mamba.

Green Congo mamba

Mambas are the most poisonous snakes in Africa. The green Congo mamba lives in trees, where it can stalk its prey unseen. Green mambas eat small mammals, lizards, birds, and even birds' eggs. When the mamba is close enough to its prey, it strikes with lightning speed. Poison is injected into the victim by two large fangs in the mamba's mouth. Like other snakes, the mamba often flicks its tongue in and out. The snake is actually tasting the air for the scent of prey, predators, or a mate.

Anaconda

The anaconda grows up to 30 feet long and can eat animals as big as crocodiles and jaguar. Anacondas lie in wait at the bottom of murky pools and ambush small deer and other mammals that come to drink. An anaconda kills by coiling its body around its prey and squeezing. Anacondas dislocate their jawbones to swallow very large prey and then sleep for several days while digesting their meal. The female anaconda gives birth to live young that are smaller versions of the adult.

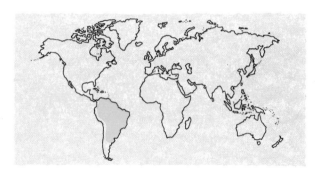

The dark patches and markings on its body help this anaconda blend in with its surroundings. ▼

Amphibians

More than three quarters of the world's frogs and toads live in rain forests. The damp conditions are ideal for these water-loving **amphibians** because they must keep their skin moist. Frogs and toads eat a wide range of small animals, and some may even eat other frogs.

Barred leaf frog

The barred leaf frog has a suction pad on the end of each of its toes. These pads help it cling to smooth leaves and to land when leaping from one leaf to another. The female frog protects her eggs by wrapping them in leaves that are hanging over water. She keeps the eggs moist by emptying water over them from her bladder. When the eggs hatch, they fall into the water below, where the tadpoles develop into frogs.

▲ The barred leaf frog has long back legs, which are good for climbing or leaping to safety.

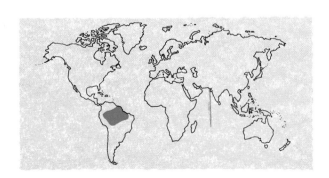

Poison arrow frog

Poison arrow frogs are brightly colored to warn other animals that their skin is poisonous. This protects them from the monkeys, birds, and snakes that eat frogs. The female frog lays her eggs on land, and the eggs are guarded by the male. When the eggs hatch, the tadpoles are carried to water on the male's back. They develop into tiny frogs in the water. The tadpoles are not harmed by the adult's poisonous skin.

▲ The American bullfrog spends much of the time near water. Unlike frogs that live in tropical rain forests, it may **hibernate** in winter.

American bullfrog

The American bullfrog lives in many parts of North America, including the temperate rain forests. This large frog can reach 6.5 inches in length and eats insects, small mammals, small fish, and even other frogs. The bullfrog can inflate its body with air, making it look even larger and more fearsome to its predators. Bullfrog tadpoles are also large, feeding on algae and dead animals found in the water. The tadpoles take two years to develop into young frogs.

▲ Some South American Indians still use poison from these frogs on blow darts, which they use to catch food.

Invertebrates

Rain forests are alive with invertebrate animals, often known as minibeasts. These include snails, leeches, centipedes, spiders, and a wide variety of insects such as ants. Many invertebrates play an important role in rain forest life by recycling dead leaves into nutrients for trees and plants.

Pink-toed tarantula

The pink-toed tarantula is a large spider that lives on the bark of tree trunks. The tarantula injects poison from two large fangs into invertebrates and other small animals. This spider's predators include small mammals, birds, frogs, and lizards. If attacked, the pink-toed tarantula will scrape sharp, pointed hairs off its back and propel them at its attacker. Although the tarantula is well known as a poisonous spider, it rarely bites humans.

◀ The tips of the pink-toed tarantula's eight legs have special hairs for climbing smooth leaves.

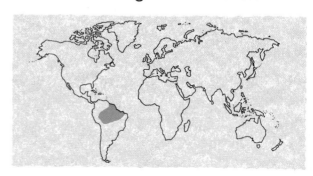

▲ Army ants travel in a column like a long, black river and may take several hours to pass by.

Leaf-cutter ant

South American leaf-cutter ants live in underground nests on the forest floor. A **colony** of ants contains worker ants, soldier ants, and a queen. The worker ants travel to nearby trees and cut leaves into pieces with their jaws. The pieces of leaf are carried back to the nest, where they are chewed into smaller pieces. The leaves are not used for food but are spat out and used as a compost to grow special fungi that will feed the entire ant colony.

As the leaf-cutter worker ants collect leaves, they are protected from danger by the larger soldier ants. ▼

Army ant

Army ants travel through the forest searching for invertebrates, lizards, and young birds to eat. Developing ant **larvae** are carried by the worker ants. A scent given off by the larvae stimulates the ants to march. When the larvae become **pupae,** they stop giving off the scent, and the ants stop marching. They form a living nest with chambers and passageways where the pupae become adult ants. The queen lays new eggs, which quickly hatch into larvae. These give off the special scent, and the ants resume their marching.

I nsects are the most varied group of animals in the rain forest. Some types blend in with their surroundings by mimicking plants; some are bizarre; while others are simply beautiful. Rain forest insects include giant beetles, wasps, flies, grasshoppers, and brightly colored butterflies and caterpillars.

▲ The female mosquito sucks up blood through a tube mouth.

Mosquito

The tiny mosquito is probably the most disliked of all the rain forest insects. This is because the female bites mammals, including humans, and drinks their blood to provide food for eggs inside her body. She finds her prey by detecting the carbon dioxide that they breathe out. Although a mosquito bite is irritating, the danger comes from the disease called malaria that is spread by the female. The female lays her eggs in water. Wriggling larvae hatch from the eggs and pupate before becoming adults that leave the water and fly. The male mosquito is harmless and feeds only on nectar and plant juices.

▲ The male morpho butterfly is more brightly colored than the female.

Morpho butterfly

One of the largest and most beautiful butterflies is the morpho butterfly. It spends most of its time in the sunlit canopy feeding on nectar from forest flowers. Butterflies and other nectar-loving insects help to pollinate flowers by carrying pollen from one flower to another. Although the tops of the morpho butterfly's wings are colorful, the undersides of its wings are drab.

Orchid mantis

One of the strangest of the rain forest insects is the Malaysian orchid mantis. The color and shape of this insect's body mimic the petals of an orchid. The mantis sits perfectly still, pretending to be a nectar-rich orchid. As an insect comes to feed, the mantis grabs its victim with its large, spiny front legs. The strike is fast and accurate, leaving the insect very little chance of escaping.

▲ The Malaysian orchid mantis is strange, beautiful, and deadly.

Glossary

Algae Very small plants with no roots, stems, or leaves. They live in water or damp climates.

Amphibians Cold-blooded animals that live both on land and in water.

Camouflage The way in which an animal hides itself from an enemy, changing its body shape or color to blend into its surroundings.

Canopy The tallest layer of trees in a forest.

Carnivores Animals that eat meat and fish.

Climate The weather conditions of an area over time.

Cold-blooded Animals that are unable to make heat to warm their own bodies. Their body temperature is similar to that of their surroundings.

Colony A group of the same kind of animal that lives and works closely together.

Decay To rot, especially dead leaves and plants.

Emergents The tallest trees in a forest, stretching past the canopy layer in search of sunlight.

Extinct No longer existing, such as an animal or plant species that has died out completely.

Habitat An area where animals, plants, and people live. Rain forests and deserts are both habitats.

Herbivores Animals that eat only plants.

Hibernate To sleep, without waking or feeding, during cold weather.

Invertebrates Animals that do not have backbones.

Larvae Insects at the feeding and development stage after hatching from eggs.

Mammals Warm-blooded animals whose females give birth to live young, which they feed with milk from their bodies.

Monsoon Wind that changes direction with the seasons.

Nutrients Substances that are taken in by plants and animals to help them grow.

Pollinate To transfer pollen from the male part of the flower to the female part of the flower to make seeds.

Predator An animal that hunts and kills other animals for food.

Prehistoric A very long time ago, before historical events were written down.

Prey Any animal that is caught and eaten by another animal.

Pupae Insects at the stage of development between larvae and adult.

Reptiles Cold-blooded animals with scaly skins.

Vegetation The plant life of an area.

For Further Reading

Coote, Roger, ed. <u>Atlas of the Environment</u>. Milwaukee: Raintree Steck-Vaughn, 1992

Dixon, Dougal. <u>The Changing Earth</u>. Young Geographer. New York: Thomson Learning, 1993.

Gallant, Roy A. <u>Earth's Vanishing Forests</u>. New York: Macmillan Children's Books, 1992.

Hare, Tony. <u>Rainforest Destruction</u>. Save Our Earth. New York: Franklin Watts, 1990.

Lessem, Don. <u>Inside the Amazing Amazon</u>. New York: Crown Publishing Group, 1995.

Tesar, Jenny. <u>Endangered Habitats</u>. Our Fragile Planet. New York: Facts on File, 1992.

Notes About Habitats

The world is divided into various habitat types, including rain forests, temperate forests, grasslands, deserts, mountains, and oceans. The distribution of these habitats is partly determined by the topography of the land and partly by the climate. Together, these help shape the face of the planet. A way of classifying habitats is by the amount of rainfall they receive.

In some parts of the world, these different habitats have distinct borders, for example, when a forest meets the sea. However, it is more common for habitats to blend slowly into one another. Consequently, some animals may be found in more than one habitat: Leopards may be found in rain forests and grasslands, and birds of prey may soar over various habitats searching for food.

Index